Published by Urban Front

1st Edition

Graphic Design – Victoria Bowcock and Lisa Gomm

Project Editor – Christopher Morris

ISBN 978-1-9998725-0-2

Printed and distributed by Latimer Trend
latimertrend.com

Front cover photograph – Andy Stagg

DOOR COUTURE

A unique perspective of contemporary door design

ELIZABETH ASSAF

FORWARD

Here is a book that many architects and designers have been waiting for, perhaps not even aware that they were waiting, about the most important part of any new contemporary home: the front door.

Elizabeth Assaf has such detailed knowledge of how best to create a dramatic, welcoming, private, interesting or simply dynamic entrance through her detailed involvement with architects, designers and homeowners, that her advice can be relied upon whether in regard to quality, making a statement, selecting the right look or establishing the right balance between privacy, security and aesthetics.

I have known Elizabeth for almost ten years, since I discovered her company Urban Front, set up with husband Nabil in 2003, whilst looking for a pivot door for my own newly designed eco home. Having trawled the internet I was more than a little delighted to find that the best looking and highest quality doors were made in a factory only three miles from my home.

The welcome which I received, the guided tour of the factory's technical and construction process – which demonstrated the fabulously considered and executed fabrication – the enthusiasm and craftsmanship of the team, and my wonderful stylish door which looks as good as new nine years on, is yet more reason for me to entice you to read this master guide by a true artisan specialist supplier.

My practice has frequently recommended these doors to clients, who are all equally delighted with the in-depth knowledge that Elizabeth imparts so helpfully as with the end product.

Take a look through the book and you will be amazed by the impact and subtlety that can be procured through the right choice of door. The affect not only to the exterior of a property but on the interior is far more important than many of us appreciate. Choice of design, material, colour, context, placement, ironmongery and texture can all affect the end result, and this carefully considered and beautifully presented book takes us through a stunning selection route, mixing education and delight in equal measure.

This is one of those publications that you will reach for time after time, and wonder how you ever managed without it before. The fact that its reading will also count toward CPD points is a useful cherry on top of a perfect professional cake. I urge you to buy it and you will never look at your front door in quite the same way again!

JANE DUNCAN

RIBA president 2016 - 2017
Principal, Jane Duncan Architects

INTRODUCTION

ELIZABETH ASSAF

This book is dedicated to Nabil, my extremely supportive husband and co-founder of Urban Front and my two children Sahara and Raphael. Thank you for being so patient as I worked my way through this adventure of doors!

Twelve years ago I would never have thought doors would be such a large part of my life. I have spent countless nights dreaming about them in every shape and form; trying to find solutions to design issues and sometimes an array of haphazard entrances just pass through my head. During the last decade of manufacturing doors, as one half of Urban Front, I've learnt a tremendous amount from trial, error and perseverance.

The aim of this book is to be educational and help you make the most suitable choices while you embark on your door design journey. Thinking of every possible scenario may not be your way of designing a door or entrance, but I hope there is enough illustration and detail in this book to inspire you to make it the best it can be.

Those of you who are designers and architects should find enough practical information to wet your technical appetite, however the book should be easy to navigate for anyone who has an interest in contemporary design, doors or architecture.

As you read through the chapters, there is information that helps you consider all the elements that could affect the design and practical usage of a door. It encourages you to think about the technical and design aspects, while taking into consideration lifestyle and performance. I touch on subjects as diverse as doors on developments and in hallways, finishes and surface design in addition to security, door furniture and whether you should have a letter box.

Our photographer has been all over the UK and beyond to showcase these beautiful projects and their doors, to find out more you will find details about each project at the back of the book.

I hope that this book inspires you to conquer any front door or entrance dilemma!

CONTENTS

CHAPTER SIX

CHAPTER ONE
MAKING AN ENTRANCE

MAKING AN ENTRANCE

THERE IS SOMETHING TO BE SAID ABOUT CREATING ENTRANCES THAT CAN DISTINGUISH ONE BUILDING FROM ANOTHER AND DETERMINE AN IDENTITY THAT LASTS THE TEST OF TIME. ENTRANCES HAVE CHANGED RECENTLY FROM SMALLER INCONSEQUENTIAL AREAS TO MORE VISIBLE AND WELCOMING ENTITIES. IF YOU NOTICE FROM THE IMAGES IN THIS CHAPTER, THE MOVE TO THIS MORE IMPRESSIVE ENTRANCE RELATES TO VARIOUS TOPICS. LET'S GROUP THEM INTO TWO AREAS:

DESIGN: CREATING AN OVERALL IMPRESSION
PURPOSE: USAGE AND REQUIREMENT

▲ Unassuming and set back, this entrance is simple and practical with zinc cladding above the door for emphasis.

▶ A frameless glass facade, a long pathway and curved wall gives this entrance everything it needs to work.

◀ Using glass and stone to highlight an entrance is clever and adds texture.

Slate cladding, a full height striking blue door with stainless steel detail and frameless glass returns, create drama and balance out of all that grey.

DESIGN: CREATING AN OVERALL IMPRESSION

The first question to ask yourself about any entrance is how it fits into the existing building design and whether that doorway/entrance could have a strong impact on the balance of that building.

Creating buildings with a main focal entrance is accomplished with aluminium curtain walling, imposing porches, sizable overhangs, glass canopies and stone pillars. Double or triple height ceilings also impose a certain style on the frontage of barns and the more lavish building. With this type of construction, the entrance is already grand and choosing a front door is easier as the whole entrance has an existing structure and purpose.

Since many buildings designs are created with an entrance in mind, some have the entrance as just a means to enter, with the weight of the house located at the back of the building. Houses situated on hills for instance, tend to have a very simple ground level entrance with only one floor visible to the front or driveway and two or more floors visible to the back. If this is the case, creating an entranceway that has impact is crucial. This doesn't take away however the need for simplicity where applicable. Simplicity can be powerful – especially when it doesn't prepare you for what lies inside.

Materials used on the outside of the building like the windows, cladding, rendering, zinc, copper and stone are also closely related to the door choice. Cladding, for example, raises its own challenges because of the way it weathers and consequently influences the final look of the building. Copper goes green and therefore the building can look altered after a few months. Windows play an important part as traditionally they are matched to the doors on the building. This has changed over time with more and braver house builders opting for a targeted and fresher look for the doors instead of a matching culture.

Making the door the only focal point on an elevation is also significantly more popular. This is usually the case on buildings which are contemporary and plain. Although this type of design needs to achieve a very fine balance – it can be very successful. In the right size, the door and especially when it isn't too balanced can be innovative and dynamic changing the perception of the building while remaining functional.

▼ Unassuming entrance doors which are simple yet effective hide a very impressive interior. The doors work well with the building and don't overwhelm it.

▶ Simple render and grey windows set the scene for an impressive entrance. The dark wood door and copper porch work together to create a 'wow' factor.

◀ A mixture of materials including glass, stone and greying cedar cladding create an interesting entrance with a softening provided in timber.

▲ In this project, the architect wanted to match the door to the zinc roof with a barcode design – contemporary look and colourway.

◄ It works wonders when the hardwood on a front door isn't matched to the external cladding. This brings attention to the area that you want your visitors to notice, the entrance and its immediate surroundings. Using a different material like stone around an entrance also creates a focal point.

▲ Rendered frontages have been very popular and in this instance the grey windows allow the doors to stand out. Using two different door designs also helps pinpoint the main entrance.

▶ Angular designs aside the timber doors here help soften the building and the subtle use of stainless steel in the door creates the focal point.

▶ The main focus of the frontage is the door due to the amount of glass. Here the owners matched the door to an internal ceiling to soften the concrete flooring and glass throughout and allow the green from the surrounding forest to create atmosphere.

▶ The whole main entrance here is clad in timber with the front door painted in a soft grey. The eye is immediately drawn to this door allowing the cladding to emphasize the doors importance. In addition, the building is a darker shade of grey adding weight to the choice of colour for the front door.

Stone, wood and grey steel work in unison to create an attractive entrance combining both garage and front doors. Using a darker wood and stainless steel detail to contrast to stone can create a more contemporary feel.

PURPOSE: USAGE AND REQUIREMENT

There may be critics among the readers of this book who will comment that the purpose of any main entrance door is more than clear. However, the requirements of the client are wide and varied so the door design should reflect this.

Although a main entrance is 'just as it says on the tin', some clients may not use the door for more than show, or may enter the building through a garage or back door depending on their parking arrangements. Many homeowners have gates, boot rooms or multiple side entrances that dictate the design and usage thereafter.

The varied requirements for a front door could be to:

- Use as a business entrance

- Hide a room, closet or part of a room

- Fit into a predetermined building design element example: aluminium curtain walling/cladding/frameless glass

- Comply with building or conservation regulations example: Passive House or a style of door determined by regulations

- Meet certain requirements for a type of room or segregation of a room into two parts for example: pool or steam room entrances

- Fulfill security, fire exit, automatic entry and/or electric latch requirements

◀ The door in this case brings in the dark tone of the copper cladding and helps make the door stand out yet still match. A stylish and simple door solution.

◀ In this project, the link between the two buildings had to hold the small passive certified front door. Using Iroko cladding for this link is a great way to point out that it's the entrance and gives it identity.

▶ This front door is the perfect partner to this overbearing tall glass window. Few door sets would look right next to such an imposing piece of glass but in this case they've got the right balance and keep it simple.

▼ Choosing a style of door that isn't necessarily of the era is an interesting way to create interest. Art Deco mixed with a Victorian facade works for the urban setting. The door and its side panel are also hiding an internal closet.

Matching a hardwood front door to a striking red brick is tricky, a simple design in Iroko blends beautifully and doesn't take away from the impressive architecture.

▲ Choosing a unique design can help the door stand out: in this case a slither of glass between the door and side panel. By making sure the finish chosen not only complements the building but also draws attention to the entrance, an all white and grey exterior will help the door pop.

▶ Occasionally, it is essential to fit in a front door in a small area. The design tries to lead away from this issue by linking the lines on the door to the lines in the surrounding cladding. Even if you don't have the space, giving the door some character is a good way to ensure it stands out.

▲ There is nothing extraordinarily special about this front door, however, it doesn't need to be as the exterior is already quite busy with the stone cladding, roof and various windows. Keeping it simple was the key to this frontage success.

◀ It's a good idea to balance the door and its side lites with the windows on the frontage as well.

▼ Using a darker wood introduces warm tones where the majority of the frontage is grey, white and beige. The glass canopy also creates interest.

▼ Combining an Oak front door with the cladding on the roof light is a cunning trick to bring all the materials together.

Highlighting the front door with a colour, is an easy trick when you have a building totally covered in timber cladding. There is no need to match to the window colour either, as you are assured the door has prominence with it's own individual colour.

CHAPTER TWO
DOORS IN HALLWAYS

DOORS IN HALLWAYS

BY DEFINITION, HALLWAYS ACT AS A PASSAGE FROM THE ENTRANCE OF A HOUSE TO THE REST OF THE LIVING AREAS. HOWEVER, THIS GENERALLY OVERLOOKED SPACE HAS PROGRESSED OVER TIME AND SEEMS TO HAVE GAINED A MORE GLORIFIED STATUS DESPITE BEING JUST A WALKWAY.

CHOOSING FRONT DOORS SHOULD BE ALL ABOUT THE EXTERNAL ELEVATION AND NOT THE INSIDE OF A HOUSE BUT GIVING THOUGHT TO HOW A DOOR AFFECTS THE HALLWAY IS A GOOD PLACE TO START FOR ANY DESIGNER.

There is no better way to create a frame for your view than recreating a hallway like this one. Using cladding throughout the hallway creates a tunnel-like effect drawing all attention to the view, and sets the scene for that glass ceiling and the amount of sky that is visible. The clever storage within that cladding also keeps this space practical.

▼ Combining doors of different finishes
is a great way to emphasise their importance
in a hallway. Here the storage in the hall has
white glossy doors and the door into a room is
in American black walnut in a matt finish. The
internal door matches the front door but leads
the eye to the door that is in constant use.

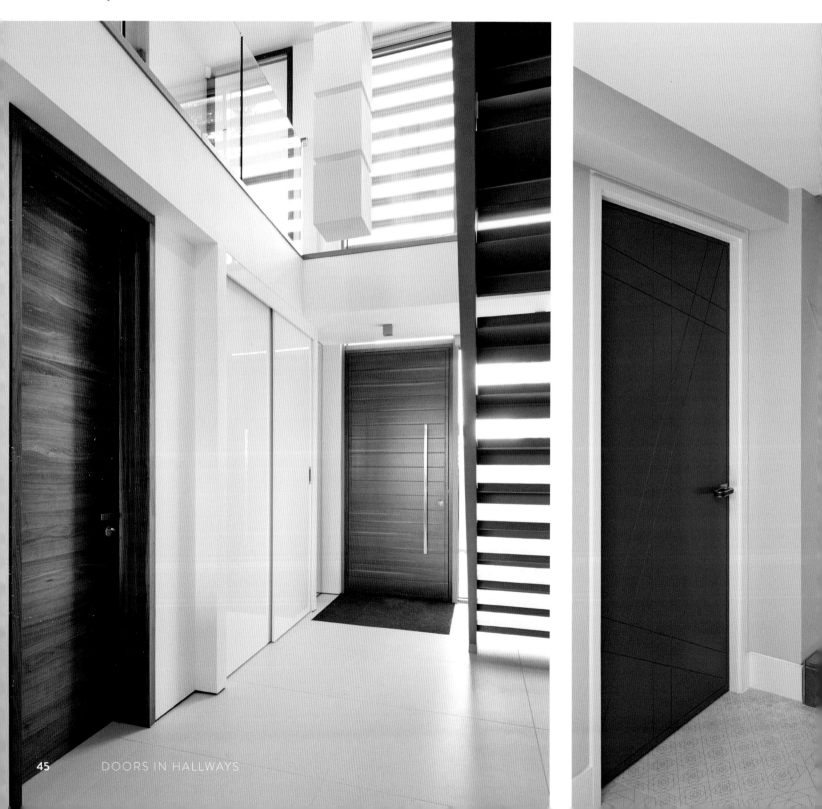

▲ The choice of wood and design for the front door on this house sets a tone of Scandinavian design and simplicity. The furniture, flooring and the white internal door also allow for the door to have its own wow factor and identity. In particular, with the door having a side boarded panel and not a glass side lite, makes it feel larger without being large.

◀ The mix of materials here work so well: geometric flooring, a flowing lined door and a concrete staircase all combine to create a contemporary but classic feel. Using a darker colour on the door itself and not on the frame also creates drama.

◀ Creating a frame for your front door within a glass architectural wall creates drama and frames the entrance. Although the rest of the hall is simple, the striking chandelier and the colour of the door is light yet very effective in achieving a 'wow' factor.

▶ Mixing doors of different wood species is an interesting way to give each door its own identity. Here, a Fumed Oak front door with an American black walnut internal door mixed with a panelled white door for storage oddly works. If you'd seen this on a mood board, you may have questioned the designer's inspiration. Again, creating drama doesn't have to follow the usual rules.

▶ Mixing old and new can be a struggle, but as you can see from this image, it can work if done correctly. A fairly contemporary door with an over panel to give it even more height when viewing from the outside is mixed with traditional furniture and a grandfather clock. Don't be worried about creating drama in an unusual way.

◀ Using colour to draw the eye isn't new, however, combine that with an all-white interior, a spectacular chandelier and an American black walnut staircase and you have the recipe for hallway magic. Even the concrete flooring here works amazingly well with the rest of the scheme. The amount of light in this area is also perfect.

▼ This hallway is a classic contemporary hero. Fine dark wood with a bronze handle and a marble and steel staircase keep this space classy, simple and draw attention to the elements that are of consequence.

HALLWAY MAGIC

In terms of the association of the front door to the hallway, most people only care about the design and whether it matches all the other doors in that area. There are many other issues to consider including:

The stairs and their distance from the door

This isn't just about the swing of the door (which is also essential), it also relates to allowing enough space for a wheelchair to turn, and for the return of the staircase depending on how big that is.

**Privacy and light –
affecting the internal passage**

Even if there are gates, most people don't want a clear view straight through their house. Although a lot of the more contemporary new builds are designed this way, it's not always ideal. Sandblasted, etched glass or even intelligent glass could easily solve the problem.

Yes, it is possible to flip a switch and have your glass change from clear to sandblasted in a few seconds. Commonly used internally this is great when privacy is essential. Using sandblasted glass prevents you from seeing out as well but a good compromise is having etched glass which is sandblasted glass which has some clear areas in numbers or letters.

Allowing enough practical light in is a criterion for hallways. The trend may be for bigger doors and more glass with galleried hallways and glass curtain walling, but this isn't always the case. Depending on design sometimes houses may have no way of bringing in light except through the door itself. Even a slither of a vision panel can create enough light.

Other clever ways to increase light when there is no available light source in a hall:

a. Decrease the height of a door and to include a storey lite above it.

b. Use a fully glazed door.

c. Make the vision panel a little larger (in contemporary designs these are usually quite thin)

d. If the door needs to stay solid, decrease its width to allow for a side lite even if this is thin, some light is better than none at all.

Access to storage

The use of sliding doors or moving the closet space to a more appropriate area will make sure the front door does not restrict access.

Practical hall furniture and its placement

If your client has children, it is most likely that you will need a seating area near the front door. How this will be accommodated and how it affects the swing of the door, any glass windows and the stairs is essential.

Other internal doors and how they relate

Matching the front and internal doors seems to come in and out of fashion depending on personal opinion. Whether you do or don't can highlight the front door less or more and change the dynamics of a space simply because of colour. Many prefer to match their front door to their staircase and have internal doors the same colour as their walls.

Disability access

In terms of hallways and the front door, access is fundamentally about being able to enter the front door and have enough space to turn a wheelchair. Essentially you also need to then close the door and turn the handle effectively too. Building regulations determine that there should be a minimum size to allow for wheelchair access and also a mobility threshold on the cill that allows for this. You can read more about cills and thresholds in Chapter five: Door detail.

Flooring

Matching flooring to the front door is another concern some clients have. This is not essential but seems to be a constant dilemma especially if the flooring is wood. This appears to be less of an issue when the flooring is stone, concrete or porcelain tiles.

Any building regulations like flush cills

Again another topic covered in Chapter five: Door detail but essential information to keep in mind. Cills and thresholds are of great consequence when designing and fitting a front door.

Needless to say this hallway is dramatic. The door is surrounded by glass creating a lot of light. Matching the design of the door to the internal doors and using a contemporary chandelier directly in the entrance is a great way to emphasise the importance of this area. Note how the door colour doesn't match the floor, but the door still works very well.

▶ Hallways often lead into open plan spaces and the trick is to keep a flow that feels effortless. Even a change of flooring here doesn't affect the feeling. The front door matches the hall flooring and then also matches the kitchen furniture. A clever way to bring everything together is making sure there is continuity between your doors, furniture and your flooring. A splash of yellow doesn't hurt either!

◀ European Oak is a warm hardwood and is a skilful way of warming up an all-white interior. This hallway is also a good example of just the right amount of space to allow for the door to open and for someone to be standing comfortably behind it.

▶ What's not to like? This room ticks all the boxes for contemporary, stylish, and dramatic without compromising on light and space; through the simple use of a white patterned door in an all-white room with lots of glass and small highlights of dark wood.

▼ High ceilings in hallways allow for lots of light and drama which can be even more special using large pieces of artwork and a chandelier.

▼ Link hallways are quite hard to do using glass, and a very big door is a way to improving the overall atmosphere. In this hallway, a glass square in the floor allows you to see into the basement.

◀ As you would have noticed, stairs feature heavily in the images in this chapter and can take up a lot of space in hallways. How they sit with the front door is an essential part of design. This front door in European Oak, with stainless steel strips, is framed by a boarded panel and a side lite to create a structure that line up the stairs perfectly.

▼ Another good example of mixing hardwoods. European Oak and Fumed Oak mix well in this hallway that is divided by a load bearing wall. The dark wall surrounding the stairs brings the two kinds of wood together and doesn't dampen the amount of light available.

This full height door dominates the entrance to this extension and here lies the beauty. All that glass needed an anchor and the door fits the bill perfectly.

CHAPTER THREE
TIMBER CHOICES

TIMBER CHOICES

FINDING AND DECIDING ON A FINISH FOR A DOOR CAN BE THE HARDEST PART OF THE PROCESS. NOT ONLY IS IT PERSONAL. IT ALSO SETS THE FINAL LOOK AND FEEL OF THE FRONTAGE AND HOW A DOOR WILL APPEAR FROM THE INTERIOR HALLWAY. THE 'PERFORMANCE' OF THE FINISH OR TIMBER CHOICE IS ESSENTIAL FOR MAINTENANCE AND LIFESTYLE MAKING THE CHOICE NOT ONLY VISUAL BUT OPERATIONAL.

European Oak flush door and side panel
– a perfect example of warming up an
entrance when there is a lot of white
render and cool greys.

HARDWOOD

Hardwood easily warms up a stark exterior and blends in with plenty of different facades. The beauty of hardwood is that is not only versatile but changeable over time. When first cut, timber starts off with an initial colour and this changes many times over its lifespan. Understanding the specifics and features of a hardwood before making your choice can manage your expectations and prepare you for its natural transformations. Identifying how much maintenance a wood requires is essential – no one likes the surprise of unexpected work.

The most popular hardwood for doors:

European Oak
One of the most popular choices in the UK is European Oak. It is well-liked due to its great maintenance features and the fact that it endures well over time; retaining its deep golden colour and becoming more beautiful as the years go by.

Sapele
Used widely in the UK, Sapele is a cheaper hardwood compared to some of the more popular options with a deep mahogany colour, lending itself more to a traditional look, it maintains well and has a moderate durability.

American Black Walnut
A good classical choice that works well in both traditional and contemporary dwellings, American Black Walnut is one of the popular choices for those who want a darker finish. It isn't as good as Oak for maintenance and durability as it requires more protection than most woods.

Iroko
When freshly cut, Iroko has a distinct yellow colour and only changes to a golden brown when exposed to light. With excellent strength properties, it compares well with teak; although weaker in bending and compression and is commonly used as an inexpensive alternative. With a medium texture and small moisture movement, it is used mainly for exterior joinery.

Fumed Oak
With colour ranging from deep brown to honey-brown, Fumed Oak is a beautiful hardwood. These colours coupled with intense blonde streaks (these occur in the secondary process of fuming) keep it dark and intense. With similar structural properties to European Oak in its durability, the fuming process gives it that much more character.

Cedar
Western Red Cedar is renowned for its variation in colour, ranging from chocolate brown to reddish brown and salmon pink; although the main colour is reddish brown. It is quite a soft hardwood and known for its use as cladding.

◄ American black walnut is more well known for its use in furniture but makes a good choice for a door too.

▶ An oak stained ebony door with just the right amount of pigmentation to highlight the door in comparison to the flint wall and burnt cedar cladding.

▶ Wood and stone work very well together and particularly if the stone is light and the wood is in dark contrast.

FINISHING HARDWOOD

The most popular way to finish hardwood is to either oil or lacquer the door and both depend on how much maintenance you would like to do over time.

Here is a list of Pros and Cons to help you make that all important decision.

1. Although oiled doors look natural and beautiful, the downside is that they need regular reapplication. This depends on which side of the house your door is on and if there is an overhang or porch over the door. You will need to apply oil every 6-8 months or possibly once a year, if the door is set back and doesn't get any sun or rain. Oiling is quite simple and anyone can do it which is something to weigh up when trying to make that decision.

2. It's also worth noting that hardwoods change in colour depending on their finish. An oiled Iroko will go darker, but in contrast Wenge or Fumed oak doors will become lighter. Walnut will initially go darker and then blonde in the sun over time. So, this will have a big impact on how you'd like the door to look in the future.

3. Some clients don't oil or lacquer their doors because they want them to grey. In this case, you would use an antifungal oil that would protect the wood but not allow it to keep its colour. This is definitely a way forward for a more contemporary look and feel.

4. Lacquered doors can look less natural and have a slightly satin sheen, but can, depending on their situation in the house, last anywhere between 4-6 years without any maintenance. Doors on houses by the sea and houses that face the elements on the frontage would probably need maintaining more often.

5. If you have cladding on your house, the finish can determine what type you choose for the door. If you are going to allow the cladding to grey and don't want the door to match, then it's a good idea to be creative and go for something totally different. But, if they are going to match, lacquering may be easier as it requires less maintenance.

6. Occasionally the interior design of the house can determine which finish will be a better match to a floor or staircase.

Unfinished Hardwood

Hardwood doors which are under a canopy or protected properly with anti-fungal oil can also be a finish option. The popularity of this natural look, which leaves doors slightly greying, can work very well on certain buildings. With a good understanding of the maintenance and how this look can affect 'performance', it is certainly achievable.

◀ Oiled fumed Oak brings out
the dark beauty of this hard wood.
Simple yet elegant.

▶ This lacquered fumed oak is
light and stripy creating
a striking effect.

Metallic

The trend for metallic doors has exploded in the last few years and seems to have passed the point of being a fad. With this new finish available on doors, the need to clad a door in metal sheets is no longer necessary. Metallic finishes are essentially a paint containing powdered metal – it oxidises over time just like typical metal. This finish provides an opulent alternative and can bring together various finishes where standard paint or hardwood wouldn't work.

A 'wow' door that adds character and beauty. A pretty unique alternative to the warmth of wood.

Painted

Doors that are painted require a lot less maintenance, which is why the majority of people choose this finish. Other reasons can be for the purpose of design (certain houses look better with a painted door), adding colour and matching windows. Paint requires maintenance only every 4-5 years depending on exposure. It also works very well with timber cladding frontages, stone and white render.

▲ A standout colour keeps the look contemporary and adds interest.

◀ Using a green colour here was an emotional choice for this homeowner whose mother loved this colour.
This works well matching to the flint wall and the grey cladding.

Staining

Most hardwood doors have traditionally been stained. It isn't always considered by designers as the most effective way to finish because it disguises the original hardwood and changes the overall look. The benefits are many though as staining provides better protection from UV light, if done correctly, and can be cheaper than buying the more expensive darker woods. Another benefit is being able to see the grain of the hardwood – so that even a door stained grey still has visible grain beneath.

▶ Double teak stained Iroko doors with stainless steel detail make for an impressive entrance.

◀ Grey stain on oak elevates this door to another level keeping the grain and creating colour.

▶ Ebony stain on Iroko stands out in an all beige hallway.

Wood choices

iroko

western red cedar

fumed oak

american black walnut

european oak

sapele

▶ Kebony is treated hardwood which weathers exceptionally well. Here a house is cladded entirely in Kebony with a simple matching door.

CHAPTER FOUR
SURFACE DESIGN & CONFIGURATION

SURFACE DESIGN

DESIGNING A DOOR CAN BE A FUN BUT
TOUGH JOB. ACHIEVING SIMPLICITY AND
CREATING A DESIGN THAT FLOWS WITH
MIGHT, TAKES TIME AND DEDICATION.
INSPIRATION COMES IN DIFFERENT FORMS
AND ALTHOUGH MANY THINK A DOOR
SHOULD BE INSPIRED BY THE BUILDING
IT'S GOING ON, IT'S OFTEN THE CASE
THAT A DESIGN OR FASHION OBJECT OR
EVEN NATURE IS WHERE THE VISION AND
CREATIVITY COME FROM. WE WILL LOOK
AT SOME OF THE ELEMENTS THAT MAKE A
DESIGN SUCCESSFUL IN THIS CHAPTER AND
WHAT COULD HELP STIMULATE
THAT PROCESS.

This wavy design evolves from straight lines and creates an elegant and fluid design.

◀ Grooving a door in a haphazard pattern and using decorative stainless steel strips can add interest. You will note the different colours of the Iroko here which also add to the overall design.

▶ You shouldn't be afraid to mix materials. Note that this house has two types of stone, copper and this striking front door with its stainless steel panel and glass which adds interest and still works well with the property.

In the past, certain manufacturing processes limited the design of hardwood doors. Designers now have the opportunity to be imaginative, even when considering the performance of the door, due to developments in the lamination process. Doors with raised elements can cause issues with water ingression so making sure you are designing a door suitable for the elements is key.

Designing a door depends primarily on the end result you are trying to achieve. Here are a few options:

- Disappearing design: for example, a door that matches cladding so that the door isn't immediately visible. A more popular option for contemporary design where simplicity rules and there is no need for an obvious doorway.

- Statement design: a door that stands out can become a 'wow' factor on any house. To achieve this it may be a design with detail that is striking.

- Architectural design: Some houses with distinctive detail like zinc cladding, particular shaped roofs or standout bricks need a door that works alongside them.

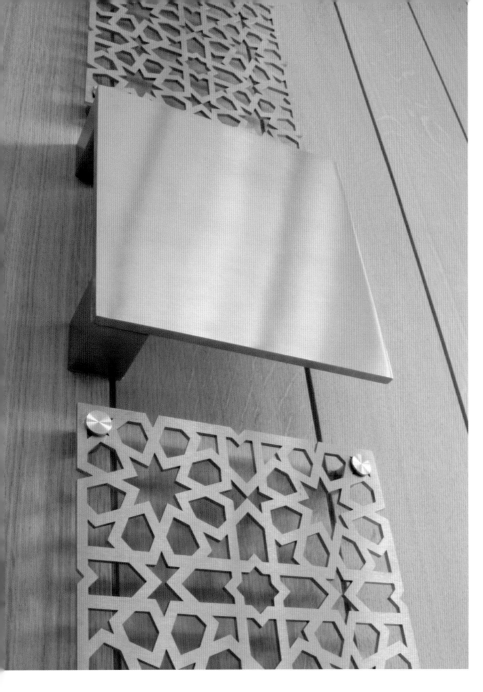

▲ Geometric stainless steel cut out panels on this door can be more of an accessory than an actual surface design. However, they are fixed and dramatically change the way the door looks. This is also a good example of taking into account how the design could affect the performance. By raising these panels from the face of the door it prevents the wood behind them from rotting due to water ingression.

One way to achieve these is by adding detail on the surface.

Grooves specified on CAD and then cut using a CNC are the easiest way to produce design on a door. Creating style is another process altogether and can include adding a certain amount of detail or better still not adding detail to a design to keep it effortless and effective.

Detail that can be added:

- Vertical and horizontal grooving, angled or wavy grooves

- Inserts: stainless steel, corian or leather

- Glass in the form of vision panels

- Mixing materials: for example, wood and metal together

- Adding accessories to 'complete' the design: see information in Chapter Door detail.

You can see examples of the above in some of the images in this chapter, the captions go into a little more detail about each choice of surface design.

Door design that stands the test of time is what every building needs. Yes, trend dictates a lot of the new products we see today, but to be timeless a door should be there 30 years later and not look dated. To achieve this, simplicity is key even when a sensational design is needed. Below is a list of some of the areas on a building you can use for taking inspiration for a door design:

- Cladding: stone, timber, zinc or even architectural cladding

- Shape: of the building, windows, roof

- Environment or location of building: seaside or in a forest or a city (urban influence)

- Building Materials: like bricks, windows, roof linings etc

You can see a few examples of this here.

▲ Red corian and stainless steel strips are the products used here to emphasise the shape of the British flag. A daring way to get a message across and a fantastic illustration of mixing materials and how anything can be inspiration for surface design.

Producing new designs by **taking inspiration from historical design** can be an effective creative process. Original Edwardian or Victorian designs for example lend themselves well to being adapted so don't be afraid to take an original period design and rework it cleverly to achieve a look that works on the right building.

You can see a few examples of this here.

◀ A good illustration of both a period design reinvented and a surface design that combines steel inserts and geometry.

▶ Georgian design mixed with a contemporary edge make this door work somehow. The oval vision panel is reminiscent of time goes by but brings the door into the 21st century with straight lines and minimal detail.

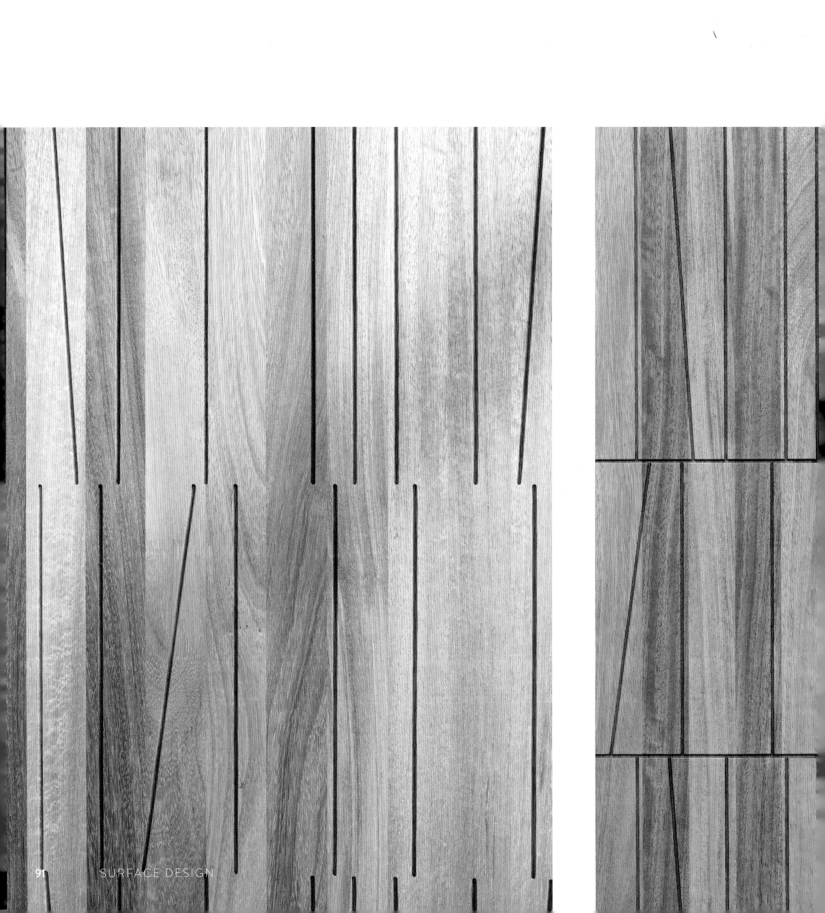

◄ These two images are a case in point for how one groove can change a design. One has horizontal lines and the other doesn't, otherwise these designs are identical. Note how much of a difference the horizontal lines make. One simple detail can catapult a design into a different league.

◀ Grooves going over two plains work well in this case. Note the detail of the groove at the escutcheon and the placement of the handle and the door viewer – all contribute to the design to complete it.

▶ A zigzag design is complemented by a matching handle. Note that the grooves of the lines don't actually meet and create a different visual than if they did. Adding a horizontal line into that zigzag only multiplies its effect.

◀ Blending doors into their surroundings is another way to create drama. This door has an element of nature to it which is the idea behind this seaside home. This little detail of stainless steel strips helps keep some glamour too.

▶ Note how the grain and texture of the wood blends well with the stainless steel and glass elements to create an attractive result.

1

2

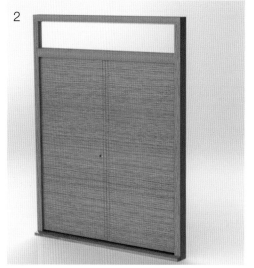

3

4

5

6

7

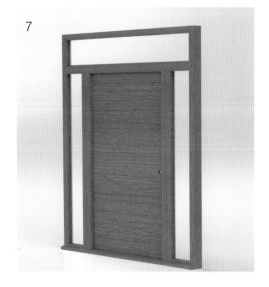

8

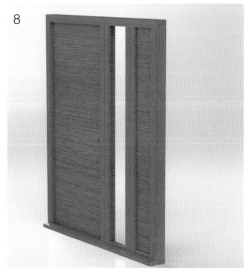

9

CONFIGURATIONS

Nearly as important as design, the way your front door is laid out can make an entrance work or fail. A front door can help balance a building from the outside especially when it doesn't have a distinct double fronted (equal windows on either side of the door) aspect. In a few instances doors are not the focal point of the frontage and may be hidden to the side or back, yet they still need to blend well and work to the benefit of the dweller in terms of how they are used.

In the illustrations opposite you will find some popular configurations.

1. Simple door and side lite

2. Double doors with a storeylite – a good way to allow light to filter through when there is no space for side lites

3. A door and a half with a side lite – this works well when there is a large opening but only one side lite is needed.

4. Door and two side lites

5. Overhead boarded panel door – suitable if it's not possible to have a full height door.

6. Boarded side panel door– used to fill in space when a wide door isn't possible, also a good way to hide hallway closets and can be used to house a letter plate.

7. Large door with two side lites and one storeylite allowing the maximum light to enter through the opening.

8. Door with side lite and a boarded side panel which is a good way to hide a hallway closet.

9. A door with two side lites on a return – a good way to enlarge/enclose a porch area, add light and create space.

How to consider the layout of your door from the inside:

1. Focus on the inside first, is there anything in the way of the door opening in a certain direction or a need to centralise the door to allow an easy flow?

2. Is there a lack of light? This may mean you need more side lites or a storeylite to allow light to filter through. This can also determine which side to have a side lite as it may be that one corner of the hallway is darker than another or that more light is needed for a staircase.

3. Is there a need to hide a closet, cloakroom, area in the hall or provide an outlet for a postbox? This will determine what side a boarded panel needs to go on if needed.

4. If none of the above are issues and anything is possible it's then a good idea to consider which way you'd like the door to open – left or right or even if it needs to be outward opening (outward opening doors are more the norm in Europe but may be needed if you have restricted space for opening the door). If you have a particular feature like a stunning staircase and you'd like that to be the first thing visitors see when they walk in, you may need to consider which way the door opens to highlight it. This can also work in reverse if you'd like to hide a particular feature from view.

How to consider the layout of your door from the outside:

1. Many are convinced that the balance of the house is the most important factor to keep in mind when configuring your front door layout. This may be true if the house is a perfect double fronted house with an equal number of windows on either side of the door and no windows above. In most cases however, this isn't the situation and you can be more creative with how the door is laid out.

2. If the house is double fronted and has windows above the door, consider the layout of those windows and try to align the door accordingly. Please note that the door doesn't have to match but may look more in tune with the building if it is aligning.

3. Some buildings have no windows to align with on the front door side, or have a haphazard frontage with extensions to the side and windows at different angles. In these cases, it would be best to start with considering how the door would stand out the most and become a focal point. The size you have to work with will best determine the layout too.

4. If an opening is large with space for more than one side lite or even multiple side panels and side lites, then consider the layout with both internal and external elements in mind. A large size could fit in two doors, or one large door with large side lites, or a door and a half with side lites.

5. One Door or More? Contemporary house design has dictated that most choose to have one large door instead of double doors, but this depends on the function of the door. It may seem obvious to most that with double doors there is always a slave door that remains closed unless needed for bringing in large furniture. There is that lovely perception (like in Hollywood movies) that one would open both doors at once but alas it isn't practical. So if a doorway is not large, opening one door would mean that only a small space is available to pass through.

6. Height and width of the door are also two elements that need consideration with layout. On more traditionally designed homes, doors usually have a storeylite to allow light in. However, you can also have a full height door with a vision panel which could achieve the same result just in an updated fashion.

The rest of this chapter has an abundance of examples of some of the layouts discussed above.

If you study this image, you'll see how the boarded panel on the side actually hides an internal closet. It also doubles up as a letter box too so that no post is falling into the hall. The side lite solves the issue of light allowing an impressive and stylish entrance.

◄ A clever way to enclose a large opening is to use cladding and divide the door from the side lite so each is a separate entity.

▶ Design and function can work well together to create a great entrance. Here instead of having a solid door and side lite, the designer opted for a vision panel in the door and a solid boarded panel. With so much light coming through the large window above it, the entrance needed no more light but benefits from a way to see out.

▶ A good option when there is a lot of glass – is to fill the whole area of the doorway with a solid door. In this case the overhead boarded panel and boarded side panel adds interest. Otherwise one door and one side panel would have sufficed.

◀ A door with glass to the side and above with a hefty frame section, adds architectural interest.

▶ Boarded panels seem to work well when combined with a lot of glass as you would have noticed in this chapter. Don't be afraid to create drama by hiding bits of the entrance from view.
A double door would have been a predictable choice here.

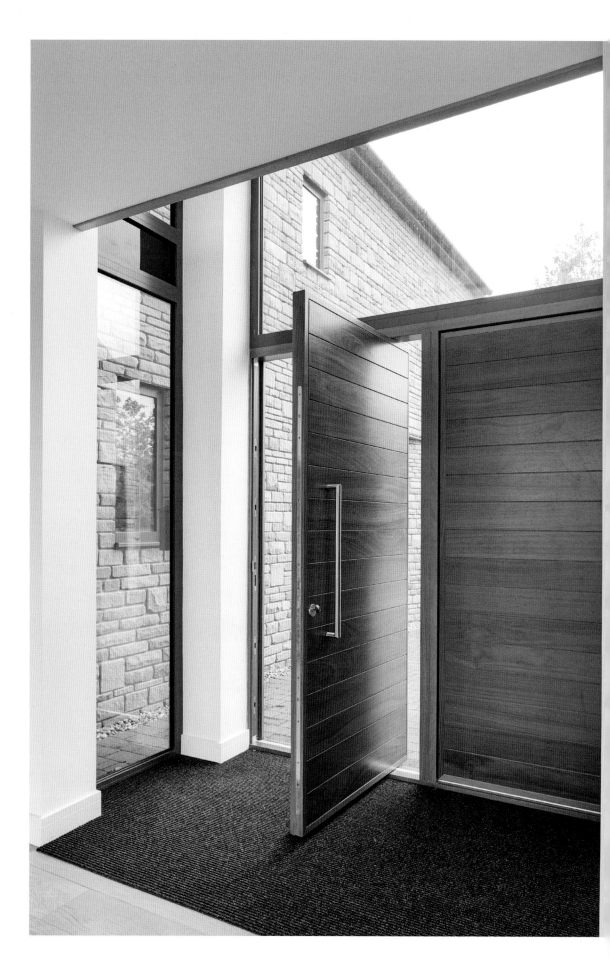

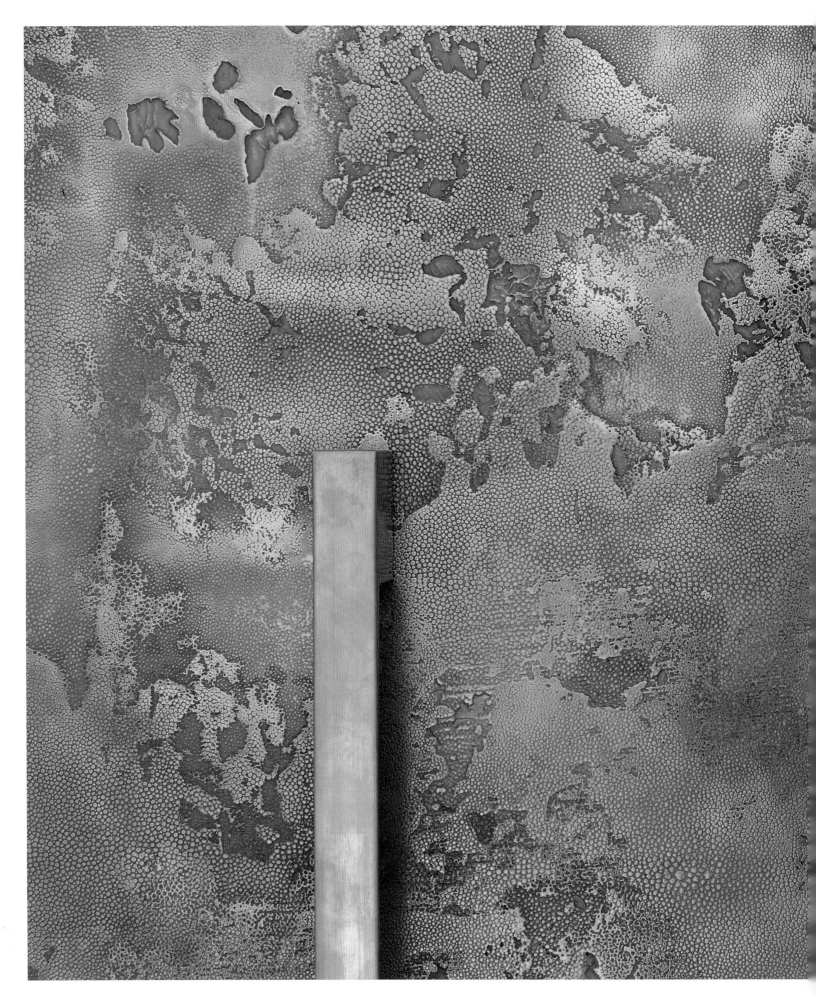

DOOR DETAIL

CHAPTER FIVE
DOOR DETAIL

DOOR DETAIL

PEOPLE FIND IT SURPRISING WHEN THEY ARE PURCHASING A DOOR THEY NEED TO ESTABLISH AND UNDERSTAND THE DETAILS THAT CREATE ITS FUNCTIONALITY AND VISUAL IMPACT.

MINIMISING VISUAL ELEMENTS HAS BEEN ONE OF MY BIGGEST FRUSTRATIONS WITH DOOR DESIGN.

BECAUSE PERFORMANCE IS SO CRUCIAL, AND IT DICTATES WHAT YOU CAN AND CANNOT DO, IT IS HARD TO ACHIEVE DESIGN SUPREMACY AND WE END UP COMPROMISING ON DESIGN TO ACHIEVE THE BEST RESULT IN FUNCTION AND OPERATION. I ALWAYS FEEL THAT ACHIEVING THE PERFECT BALANCE IS A CHALLENGE AND SO FAR HAVE NOT FOUND THE PRECISE SOLUTION TO THIS ISSUE.

THE DETAIL IN A DOOR CAN COVER ANYTHING FROM HINGES TO CILL DETAIL AND WE WILL ADDRESS ALL OF THESE ELEMENTS WITHIN THIS CHAPTER.

DOOR FURNITURE: HINGES

There are quite a few ways to hang a door and this all depends on how you'd like the door to perform for you and what you'd like it to achieve.

Side hung doors

Butt hinges are the most popular way to hang a door although not always the most attractive. Butt hinges come in various sizes to allow for the weight of the door but in recent times the 3D concealed hinge has overtaken it in popularity. This hinge is not visible from the inside when the door is closed and is adjustable in 3 directions to allow for any movement during the lifespan of the door.

The benefit of side hung hinges is that it is the best way to give you security and weather sealing. The other ways available to hang a door can never be as secure or weather tight.

Pivoting doors

Pivoted doors have become all the rage in recent years especially for the domestic market. Using hinges that allow the door to pivot from the top and bottom rather than the side adds interest to the front of any building. It is a misconception that pivots add value, as they don't, but, in this case it's all about the design and not about the performance.

The struggle with pivoting doors is the ability to create an effective seal. There will always be a small amount of space around the pivot hinge which is not totally weatherproof. In addition, pivot doors reduce the door leaf opening size and although they are generally a bigger door, they have a smaller opening. This is due to the position of the pivot hinge a few hundred millimetres from the edge of the door.

Folding doors

I have debated whether to include folding doors in this section, but I decided that folding front doors although rare do sometimes get specified due to the distance around the door and issues with space. This is more of a garage door solution but sometimes in London folding doors are specified for Mews houses.

◄ Hinged door sets allow a pretty much uninterrupted walk-through and are popular because they have the best weathering solution. With some hinges allowing a 130-180 degree full opening ability if the space for it is available.

▲ Pivot doors may not always offer the largest walk-through but they offer a special and interesting touch to an entrance.

▼ Hinges come in lots of different shapes and sizes now so choosing the correct one depends on the function needed but also of the regulations a door would need to meet. This first image shows a 3D concealed hinge which is adjustable in three directions to allow for movement in the door and is also concealed on the inside of the door. The second image shows a heavy duty butt hinge for a Passive house door which gives the best performance in terms of air leakage.

▲ Most pivoting points are 150 to 250mm from the edge of the door frame. Any closer and your walk-through is reduced. This would also defeat the purpose of the pivot.

▲ Due to the way pivot doors open, fingers could get caught between the door and the frame. Here is an example of a special rebate to help prevent this issue.

DOOR DETAIL

A hinged door set visible from the inside. A good example of concealed hinges and the clean finish they provide.

DOOR DETAIL

DOOR FURNITURE:
HANDLES

The choice of handle out there is enormous with so many possibilities available. Deciphering which is the best way to 'open a door' can be quite a big decision as it impacts on how you use your door and how you access the area in front of your home or building.

Lever handles

Lever handles work by activating the latch on a door, and therefore a door is not locked unless the lock is turned. But this also means you can access the outside of your home without having to carry a key or by leaving the door open. Lever handles for front doors are quite a traditional choice, and offer a solution that allows access to driveways/ external porch areas without locking. It is worth noting however that lever handles can look small and insignificant on a larger size door if not large enough.

Pull handles

Pull handles are a more contemporary choice and tend to be larger. They have a push and pull action that gives a more comfortable opening for a door. However, if it doesn't have a lock to hold the door on the latch, then there is no way to keep it open without a key unless a specialised lock is used which allows this.

Pull handles can also include fixed door knobs which are only used to push and pull a door and rarely relate to the latch in any way.

Handle finishes

There is a wide variety of handle finishes to choose from here is a list of the most popular:

1. Chrome

2. Stainless Steel

3. Bronze

4. Copper

5. Aluminium

6. Rose Gold

7. Coloured PVC on aluminium

8. Steel

▶ A pull handle with a kink mirrors the design of the door. Pull handles should be functional but adding a design twist can also make them a feature in their own right.

▼ A delicate handle in solid bronze prettifies an Iroko door.

◀ Lever handles are still popular in the UK for front doors choosing a sturdy and longer lever will help balance the door. In this instance, a solid bronze lever does the job.

▶ An essential part of choosing handles and fitting doors is thinking about whether there is space for the handle when the door is open. Here, this was overlooked because the frame was being hidden into the wall so an indentation had to be created in the wall to allow for the handle. Works as art in this instance.

▲ Functional accessories are definitely the future. Have a look at this handle that also doubles up as a lock. Sometimes, the handle also hides the lock and you can't even tell there is one.

▲ Choosing coloured or special finish accessories is quite a bold and stylish option. Bronze and rose gold are currently making a comeback.

▶ Be creative – a vertical handle used horizontally adds interest and automatically changes the way a door can look.

DOOR DETAIL

DOOR FURNITURE: ACCESSORIES

It might seem that I am stating the obvious, but accessories are a significant part of your entrance. Here is a list of a few of the things that you may find useful for an entrance area and make the area more practical:

The varied requirements for a front door could be:

- Doorbell or knocker

- Lighting for the door

- House name or number (as a separate accessory or can be etched into door or glass)

- Door mat

- Door stop

- Letterbox or Letterplate

- Newspaper holder

- Door viewer

Of this list, the most common query is whether to have a letterbox or letterplate.

Whether you like them or not, an essential element of any entrance is a place for a letterbox or letterplate. Your post needs to be delivered so here are some points to consider when you decide about its placement and use:

1. When letterplates are installed on your door, two things to remember are:

    The security risk: its placement too close to the middle of the door could be a security risk - enabling easy access to the lock.

    Considering the postman: Some are concerned about the postman having to bend down if they place a letterplate at the bottom of the door. This is a personal choice but letterplates look more up to date and attractive lower down and out of the way.

2. Letterplates may not be suitable for passive house or zero carbon rated houses with high insulation values because they are a source of heat loss. It is possible to buy certified letterplates however they are not always attractive or contemporary.

3. The placement of letterplates on timber door sets with grooves is important:
    If the door has vertical grooves, then the letterplate should be vertical to prevent water flowing down the door and sitting in the grooves where the letterplate is. The same applies if the door has horizontal grooves - the letterplate should fit horizontally.

4. Mail chutes are a solution but are best implemented when the building is being built as they are hard to fit after the fact. A post-box sits on an outside wall, with a tunnel through the wall with an internal basket for the post to fall into on the inside. A great option for new builds when an abundance of space is available.

5. Creating a special place for the letterplate on the door is another option and generally they fit in the side lite of a dedicated panel at the bottom or middle of the door. The benefit of this is that it is not in the door.

6. It's worth noting that if there is a clear glass side lite by your door, there is security risk if post is left on the doorstep while you are away. Would be burglars will know you are away.

7. Choosing to fit a post-box onto an outside wall, means you have to go out to collect your post but does make a lot of the above issues obsolete!! However, your post-box could also get full while you are away and alert burglars you are not around.

◀ A mail chute in a side panel is a good compromise if you don't like letterplates in doors.

▲ Be creative with your accessories. Here a
door stop is etched with the house name.

◄ Etching numbers in the door itself instead
of using an accessory, is not only an interesting
focal point for developments but reduces the
need to fit any extra items.

◀ Creating atmosphere with lighting isn't anything new but emphasizing the front door is essential to draw the eye to the correct entrance. This is the case when houses have two entrances or a favoured entrance but it lights the lock effectively and keeps intruders at bay.

Locks have come a long way in the last few years, a good example is of a self-locking 5point lock with a hold open latch option. With the flick of a small snib the lock retracts, and the door works without a lock engaging. This works well if you'd like to pop out to your driveway and not worry about carrying a key with you. Most locks would have a separate option to do this therefore cluttering up the surface of the door.

SECURITY
THE BASICS

Door security is tricky as there are so many options available to choose from. To break it down and simplify, I've concentrated on 4 main criteria your door should meet for security. Door security provides the client with peace of mind and lengthens the time it would take potential burglars to get in.

1. The door construction itself should be strong. When doors undergo tests for security, the door leaf itself is attacked with something sharp and with considerable weight. The ability of the door to withstand attack, not just it's hinges, lock and cylinder helps span out the time needed to break in.

2. The lock should meet certain regulations and protect the door not just in the centre but also in the corners i.e. top and bottom of the door.

    There are two standard types of locking, a mortice lock and multi point locking.

    A standard mortice lock will have a latch and one shooting bolt. This usually protects the centre of the door, however, if a burglar were to hit the corner furthest from the hinge and continue to do so, the lock in the centre can weaken and that is why multi point locking is useful. A 3 or 5 point lock will provide extra shooting bolts that will provide a stronger hold into the frame and therefore make it harder to weaken the lock. The bolts shoot into the frame in 3 or 5 areas providing extra security and support.

3. The escutcheon which protects the key cylinder and the cylinder itself should have security credentials.

    Key cylinders today have become extra secure with features allowing you to prevent a key from being copied without a registered pin, in addition, they should be anti-picking, anti-bumping and anti-drilling. Security escutcheons protect the cylinder further by being difficult to dislodge and prolonging the amount of time it takes a burglar to break in.

4. The hinges and frame are also important for security as they form the backbone of a door.

    The hinges can be accessed and dislodged if the frame is compromised so the frame needs to be strong and resist attack by a crowbar or a similar tool. Butt hinges can be fitted with security bolts or 3D concealed hinges are another solution. A reinforced frame made to withstand attack also prolongs the time to break into a door.

Specialist entry systems are not for everyone and depend on the way you use your home and entrance. Many entry systems are sleek and efficient. They are available in various finishes and can work well with your front door. They sometimes come mounted on the actual door internally, but the majority are used like this – placed by the door for easy access

SPECIALIST LOCKING
ENTRY SYSTEMS

Smart homes are becoming a permanent fixture now and doors aren't immune to this new trend.

So how does a door become smart? Specialist locking is the answer and it all relates to the function required. Is the client in need of opening a door remotely or simply opening a door from another floor? Are there gates or does the door need to be extra secure because of the location? Does the lock need to work with a control system accessible from a smartphone?

All of these queries will determine how and what to include for entry systems and specialist locking.

Listed below are some of the options available as optional extras by your electrician or by your door supplier:

1. **Finger print entry (also available with remote entry)**
   Often considered a trend and not a necessity, finger print entry is popular for its ability to allow you entry into your home without a key or number pad. Most systems allow the entry of 100 fingerprints and can also connect to a smartphone. You can delete fingerprints and open the door remotely.

2. **Electric latches**
   Electric latches are not the ideal option for domestic situations. They are more widely used in commercial or apartment buildings. Electric latches allow doors to open remotely through a buzzer system but the door is then only held on a latch and not a dead bolt reducing security.

3. **Motorised locking**
   Motorised locking is the more secure option to choose for opening doors remotely or from another floor especially in a domestic situation. It provides locking a latch and is available as a single or multi point lock. This option is fail-safe or fail-secure allowing either the door to lock or open automatically in case of fire or power failure.

4. **Eye retina scanning**
   At the top end of security and an expensive option, eye retina scanning is an option that more people in high powered jobs or in the public eye are planning into their security schemes. The system is wired into the main control for the property and is supposedly indestructible.

5. **Number pad or remote control**
   More commonly seen on commercial and office buildings/number pad entry systems or remote entry are pretty standard. Not so much in use on domestic buildings as other systems are becoming more popular.

6. **Video entry system**
   Some manufacturers now fit video entry systems directly into the door with a visible screen so you can see the person on the other side. These systems are also connected to your smartphone and allow you to unlock the door remotely when used in conjunction with electric latches or motorised locking.

All of these options require electrical wiring from inside the door to enable the features above to work.

DOOR ARRANGEMENT
AND FUNCTIONALITY

Frame detail

The necessity to fit doors into varying types of wall from brick to curtain walling to frameless glass implies that it's more difficult to get the frame detail correct. In reality not much has changed except perhaps the demands of the designer and how 'clean' they'd like the finish to be. This could be in terms of how the door butts up to that particular wall, or how much difference there is in thickness between the wall and door. Frames are also increasingly being hidden inside walls and behind cladding to create a simple effortless design and finish.

Cill and threshold detail

The detail specified for a cill and threshold depends on the building, its age and whether the building is a new build and building regulations are applicable. If possible, the most suitable and effective solution is for the cill to be sunk and the entrance area threshold is flush with the inside flooring. There is also the possibility of using no cill at all although providing suitable brackets to support the frame on either side would then be essential. However, this isn't always possible due to existing steps up to the door or existing driveway restrictions and limitations in the height of the flooring in relation to the outside ground area.

Due to disability access and ease of use, Part M Building (in the UK) regulations require a threshold not to be more than 15mm above floor level for any new build or extension however as stated above if the building is older and a refurbishment is taking place, it depends on the state of the existing doorway and what is possible.

Bespoke detail

One advantage of hardwood is that the design possibilities are endless with the right amount of perseverance and hard work. Below is a list of the various possibilities available with hardwood doors.

1. Additional rebates to a frame to ensure it butts up seamlessly to glass, brick or a stone wall.

2. Flush detail that allows a door to fit into external or internal cladding and creates a door and frame with no visible rebates and simple detail. Also flush over panels which give the impression of a larger door.

3. Lighting concealed in the door within a handle, or within the hardwood.

4. Concealed handles which are embedded into the door face and aren't instantly recognisable.

5. Also listed under accessories, number and letter etching in hardwood.

6. Specialist fitting of components like concealed pet flaps.

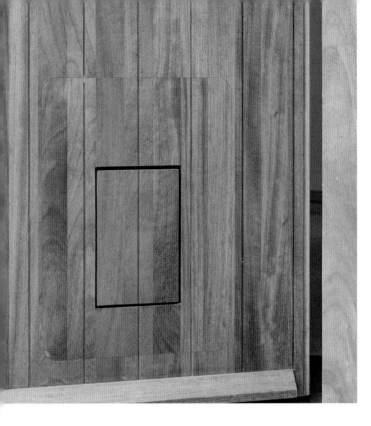

▲ It is a feat of engineering to fit such a hefty pet flap into a door and make it disappear into the surface like this. This Passive house pet flap automatically opens as the pet approaches and is secure and still sleek from the inside too.

▼ A small detail like this provides peace of mind for finger entrapment. The rebate in the frame allows child and adult fingers alike to fit in neatly.

▼ This certified Passive house doorset has a triple rebated door leaf with specialist weather sealing and hinges.

Finger safety

It may seem like a minor detail but finger safety is underestimated for doors. To prevent fingers getting trapped in or along the gap of hinged and pivot doors there is a few solutions:

1. Door finger guards which fit along the hinge

2. Finger rebates in the frame on pivot doors.

Weather sealing and weatherboarding

Everyone remembers the front doors of their childhood and the never ending drafts which meant that draft excluders were used to protect from the cold and rain. Preventing heat loss is the main job of weather seals but a doors insulation is as important to help reduce this.

New build housing that meets high levels of air tightness requires the use of double or triple weather sealing around the four sides of a door. Unbroken weather seals in high quality silicon are the best option forming a continuous and uninterrupted seal.

Weatherboards are used at the bottom of the door to allow water to run off and not settle beneath the door where the weather seals and threshold meet. These are useful when a door has little protection from the elements.

Door closers

Used for a variety of reasons from noise reduction to prevent shuddering, door closers can be an effective functional accessory.

Various door closers are also available:

1. Concealed overhead door closers which are invisible when the door is closed

2. Face fit overhead or middle of door closers which are visible on the face of the door

3. Floor pivot swing closers which are based inside a pivot hinge but require a deeper cill

4. It is also possible to have concealed free swing closers built into hinges. This option doesn't provide resistance and is a good option for rooms that are not in a circulation route.

A few of the scenarios where door closers are needed:

1. Fire doors – some are a legal requirement in Fire doors – some are a legal requirement to protect an area from fire and doors must remain closed.

2. To prevent doors from slamming i.e. reducing noise pollution.

3. Public buildings like school hallways, gymnasiums, and hospitals.

4. When doors are fitted into large glass curtain walling to prevent shuddering in the glass when the door closes.

Having a step up to the cill is pretty standard on most buildings in the UK built in the last century. The door in this image is a pivot door with a drop down seal detail at the bottom, so a raised threshold is not needed.

The majority of new buildings and extensions now have similar cills to this one. The cill is sunk to allow flush finished floor level.

◄ This pivot door has a specialist aluminium cill finishing the detail above the timber to prettify the end result. There are even lights embedded into the surface.

► A standard hinged door set with a 15mm above floor level threshold. Although there is no step here the cill doesn't finish flush.

The designer laminated two timbers together
and then used a CNC to etch through to expose
the darker timber underneath. A clever way to
achieve a visible and stunning effect.

CHAPTER SIX
SIZE MATTERS

SIZE MATTERS

IF YOU STUDY THE HISTORY OF DOORS, YOU ARE LIKELY TO SEE DOORS CHANGE IN SIZE DRAMATICALLY. DOORS WERE MADE SMALLER TO KEEP THE HEAT IN AND LARGER ON MANSIONS TO EXPRESS WEALTH. IN RECENT HISTORY DOORS HAVE BEEN THE SAME STANDARD SIZE: FOR PRICING, EASE OF FITTING AND TO BE PROPORTIONATE TO THE SIZE OF THE HOUSE. HOWEVER, CONTEMPORARY DESIGN AND ARCHITECTURE HAS SEEN AN INFLUX OF 'THE BIGGER DOOR'.

Matching the door size to the area above it creates balance.

There is no right or wrong way to size a door but there are guidelines that should help and determine why size is important.

Impact
Sizing can create visual and spatial impact, by producing a wow factor.

Space
Breaking up space imaginatively with the use of a large or smaller door, is a definitive way of creating the illusion of space and of grandeur.

Proportion
A doors size is ultimately based on proportion of the building and elements of that building. A door may seem to only take up a fraction of a structure, but its proportion holds importance due to its location and use.

To provide restrictions
Doors can be used to provide restrictions on entry. The smaller you make a door the smaller the area of entry and therefore you are restricting a pathway/entrance to a certain area.

◀ This huge house near the sea shows us 'scale' correctly. Making one face of the facade the focal point and creating a door that looks bigger than it actually is helps create a magnificent entrance.

Getting the size right may not follow a rule book but it needs some careful thinking. Here are a few areas of importance that can help improve the process and add guidance:

Door size in relation to building and the elements of the building

The best place to start with any door size would be to consider the total outline of a building, where the door is going – front, back, centre or side of a structure, and the positioning and size of the windows, garage doors, exits and driveways.

Are there any windows to either side or above the door? Doors often line up with windows to keep them in proportion and can be two or three times a window's size or even half the size of a large window. Just as it's important for a door not to be too big, it's also important not to be too small. Balancing both can be tricky but the end result can drastically change the front elevation of a house.

You may need to consider the best sizing solution if a door is being placed in a large expanse of glass or to the side of the house where it is not visible. The same applies for buildings where a door needs to be squeezed in because of other features like glass walls, cladding and garage doors. Keeping in mind the proportions of garage doors is another key point. Garage doors tend to take up at least double sometimes triple the amount of space a front door does so ensuring the door still has its place as the focal point can be challenging.

A clever way to draw attention away from a door that is too small could be to add a design feature near it to make it more distinctive or to draw the eye away from that feature.

It's not only the width of a door that can emerge as an issue. It's also the height of a door. Many older homes undergoing refurbishment, tend to have short doors due to limitations with lintels and load bearing walls. Stumpy doors aren't attractive but can be enhanced by improving the overall appearance by using vertical grooves to elongate a door when no other option is available. The same applies to making a door feel wider by drawing the eye with horizontal grooving.

◀ This door allows you to glimpse inside so you can see the sea in the background and beautiful interior. It remains a feat of engineering, the door and surrounding panels at 6 metres tall becomes a structural wall and not just 'a door'.

Glass dominated contemporary buildings leave less and less space for front doors. This image taken in summer shows how the front door becomes unnecessary, however in the winter months where the glass is always closed, a front door is more necessary. With limited space, this architect has positioned the door between two supporting columns – and on the inside a wall restricts movement to one side of the hall. See p. 161 for the internal image of this door.

Requirements for access

Door size can be dictated by access and space requirements. These restrictions sound straightforward and logical but can be missed if there are quite a few different fundamentals to reflect on.

It may be that internally there is a wall in the way, or that the door only fits in a space that is hindered by walls, supporting columns or sloping ceilings.

There could also be restrictions with staircases which can protrude into a door's opening space, or restrict a pathway and this impacts door size.

Rooms necessary to the usage of a building i.e. storage areas or cupboards that contain heating or electrical equipment are another consideration. These are often in hallways and need a certain amount of dedicated space.

Disability issues can determine whether a door needs to be motorised and possibly pivot and therefore be larger for the ease of access.

All the above can combine to limit options on a front door size and therefore the full front elevation and its final design. The images in the rest of this chapter reflect some of the points listed above and highlight the effect on a project overall.

◀ This door fits snugly between two columns and sharply to a wall dividing two areas of the house. On the outside as seen on p. 160, the door looks like it opens onto a larger area. A clever disguise when space is limited.

▶ This unusual designed house with circular and square walls is linked with a glass box and a largish front door (1.2 x 2.4m). Due to the size of the windows, the door could have potentially been larger, but this still works because it feels like a home and there is that possibility that the building could resemble a commercial building instead.

◀▼ Size is all in the perspective. This ultra-contemporary extension on a Victorian house, showcases a full height pivot door at 1.4 x 2.8m. As an added detail, the top frame is concealed in the ceiling giving it an even sleeker look. The door itself is large, but not enough to be obtrusive helping to break up all the glass walls.

Matching grooves and design on a door
to the walls of a building and to the height
of the windows can help elongate a
door and create an illusion of size. It isn't
always necessary to have a big door to
achieve the same result.

▶ Unconventional buildings can make for challenging design features. This hospital clinic is a great example of how a door can be dwarfed by glass but still achieve its purpose. There was a need for discretion in the entrance area which has been achieved by solid wood doors and etched glass windows where necessary.

Burrell
Street

Sexual Health Centre

▼ This full height entrance is domineering but the actual size of the part of the door that opens is smaller at only 2.4m high. Another illusion that works well and remains practical.

▼ This door opens up to a larger hallway, but due to wanting to include a seating area in that area, the designer needed the door to be to the side of the entrance. Although not equal to the size of the adjacent window, the door is still large and commands attention. The lesson here is that the rules may not always apply to your project and therefore doing something a little different can still work.

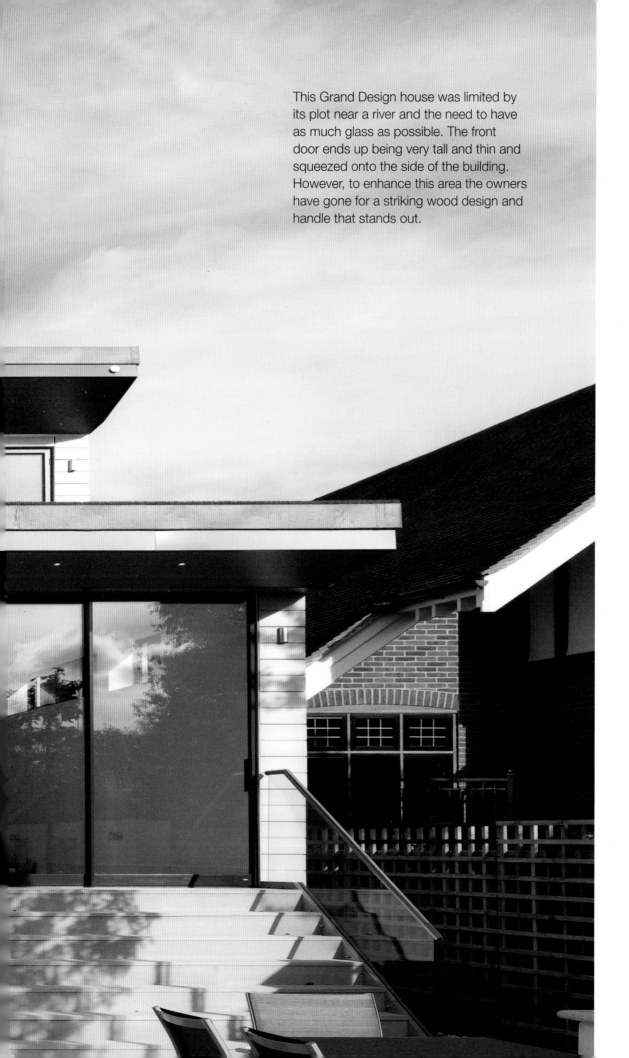

This Grand Design house was limited by its plot near a river and the need to have as much glass as possible. The front door ends up being very tall and thin and squeezed onto the side of the building. However, to enhance this area the owners have gone for a striking wood design and handle that stands out.

◄ When the top half of a building has an eye-catching roof and it could overpower the rest of the facade, choosing a door can be tricky. This designer has opted for a larger full height door in a wood matching the cladding to give the door identity. The door at 1.2 x 2.4m also matches the window on the top half of the building and lines through.

▶ Matching your front door size to the windows above is a safe way to ensure the right size. Dividing the door and side lites into 3 is a good balancing trick too.

▶ Contemporary cube houses
with various angles and wings are
a good example of the difficulty of
getting size right. This house has
a large garage door which could
dwarf the front door but doesn't
because the clever architect has
used visible columns on both sides
of the door to give it emphasis and
has also measured the door to
be about a third of the size of the
garage. Setting the garage back
has also helped the size of the
door to appear larger.

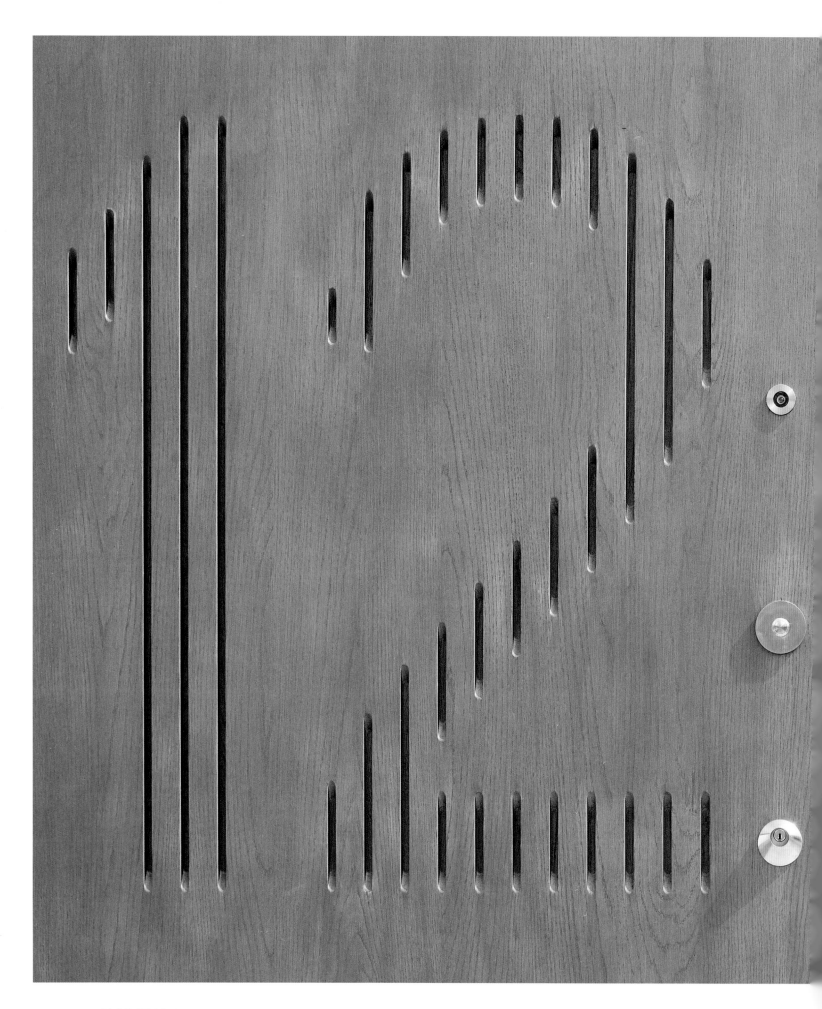

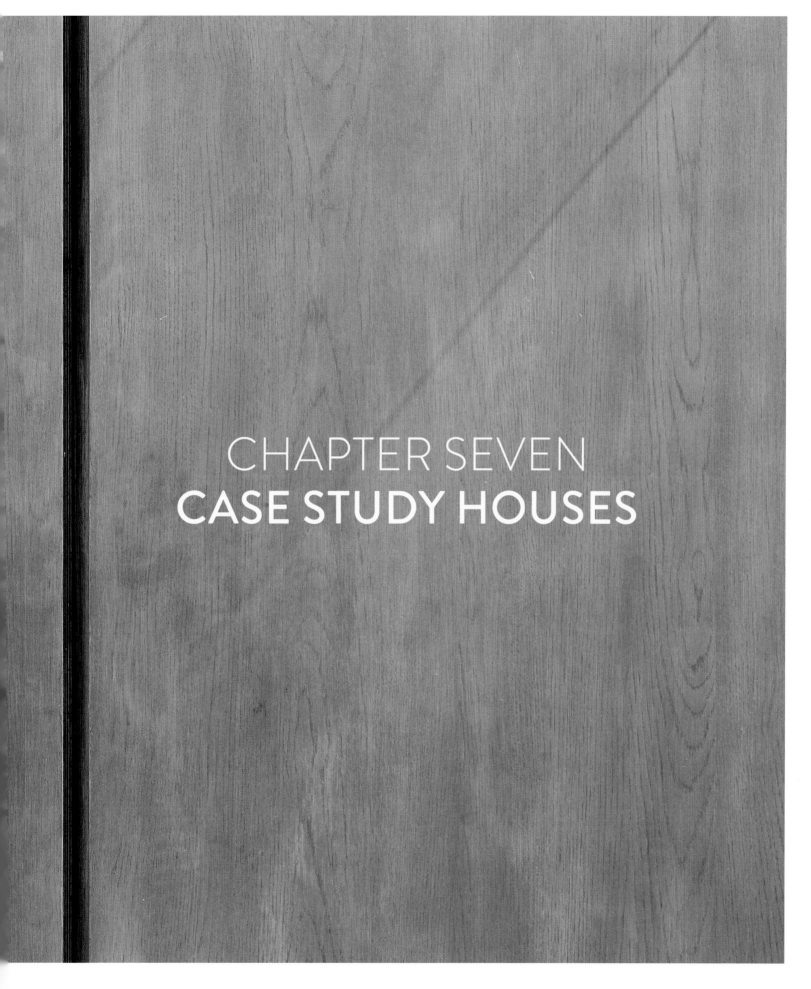

CHAPTER SEVEN
CASE STUDY HOUSES

ONYX HOUSE

CHOOSING A CASE STUDY IN THIS CASE WASN'T DIFFICULT. THE ONYX HOUSE HIGHLIGHTS MANY ISSUES THAT COULD DEVELOP WITH A FRONT ENTRANCE AND AN ANNEXE. I PARTICULARLY LIKE THAT THIS ISN'T A STANDARD RENOVATION, IT STANDS OUT AS CREATIVE AND NOT NECESSARILY TO EVERYONE'S TASTE. A DEFINITE CANDIDATE FOR 'NOT FOLLOWING THE CROWD'.

▼ Adding a glass box adds space and increases light while the pivot door draws the eye down the hall into the centre of the house.

The Entrance

So how do you create a contemporary front door on a 1930's bay window façade? Simply, by constructing a new extended contemporary version; a frameless glass box with a door as its front. Frameless glass isn't a fresh concept however if you add it to this style of house it's tricky to get right. Colour, finish and design all collaborate to determine a result that has to work or the entrance could fail miserably.

Have a look at this list of points which I believe justify this choice of entrance on this house:

- Using an onyx stain on European Oak to match in with the metallic window colour cements a contemporary edge but also brings the whole facade together.

- The ingenious number etching in the side panel breaks up a rather large area of solid hardwood without compromising the design. Going large produces a compelling effect.

- Using the door and side panel as the face of the glass box reduces visibility to the inside without reducing the light. Sandblasting only part of the glass to the sides of the box works well when viewing from the hallway.

- Keeping the door large and choosing a pivot was a good choice here due to the opening space available in the hall.

- Simple detail in the vein of the concealed handle and the door viewer show a respect for functionality without compromising design.

The Annexe

Additional doorways on facades have become more widespread with the rise of the self-build and renovation generation. Double fronted and multi-functioning houses do occasionally require two entrances; for home offices, studios, annexes or even just a side door. Getting the second entrance right is nearly as important as the main entrance because it may have more use, it shouldn't be an afterthought and it may or may not need to stand out.

How does the Onyx House achieve a successful second entrance?

- Using the same finish on the doors works it creates harmony in the facade and highlights that it's the same house not another entrance to a different house or a semi-detached house next door.

- A slightly different side panel in design and in a smaller size helps differentiate the two entrances.

- A hinged and smaller door is a standard way to reduce importance of an entrance.

- Mirroring design in a smaller version is a successful way to signal same house different door!

It's worth mentioning as I conclude this case study that entrance design is very personal, regardless of whether it works for you and your taste, can still be successful in terms of function and design.

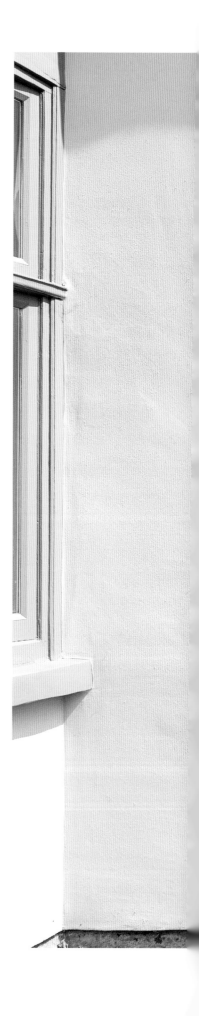

Here, the designer creates a clever illusion of space with the use of a mirror down the wall of this small annexe bedroom and with the use of a 'pretend' side panel on the outside of the annexe which in reality is hiding the bathroom. Adding a glass box adds space and increases light while here, the pivot door draws the eye down the hall into the centre of the house.

▼ Symmetry of the detail is key, a security escutcheon, doorbell and door viewer all line up in the middle door jamb and leave the rest of the door set free of accessories.

CASE STUDY

YELLOW DOOR HOUSE

IT IS UNLIKELY THAT ANOTHER HOUSE COULD DEMONSTRATE THE IMPORTANCE OF A FRONT DOOR MORE THAN THE YELLOW DOOR HOUSE. THE AMOUNT OF POSSIBLE VIEWPOINTS OF THE DOOR FROM VARIOUS ROOMS IMPLIES HOW MUCH OF AN IMPACT A SINGLE DOOR CAN HAVE.

IN THIS CASE STUDY, WE LOOK AT THE IMPLICATIONS OF COLOUR AND CHOOSING A DOOR THAT DOESN'T NECESSARILY MATCH.

Contemporary meets classic in a room where a disco ball and plants mix with a yellow door, piano, concrete floor and mustard walls. Daring and fun all highlighted further by the yellow door.

How colour can make an entrance

Yes we've seen coloured doors used on Huf Haus for years and the 60's saw a revival of bold and bright. But how does a yellow door fit in this century and beyond? This house has beige stone, dark grey brick and untreated cedar cladding plus the yellow door. Not what you'd expect could work. Without this brave colour choice, the front door would have felt overlooked.

Anything darker than yellow would have been too dark and anything lighter too pale. The house is well known in the area because of the door colour choice.

- Think of colour as functional not just visual. How can colour change the whole stance of your house and how does it impact any other houses in your street?

- A mood board for the frontage of a house is a good way to query your choices. Placing different materials together is a sure way to see what clashes in a good or bad way.

- Another way to ensure success is to think about all the materials and how they will wear over time - cladding fades into grey and stone can become dirty – will the colour have longevity?

Different lights and perspectives work dramatically in favour of the front door here creating framing that draws the eye.

The power of internal colour

Creating drama in interiors is what designers do best and this particular designer has the power of daring in abundance. Using mustard, green and coral walls in the hall to royal blue on the staircase walls and dark grey in the living room exhibit a daring for colour. Inserting a yellow door in the midst of this may seem questionable but it's successful and that is the power of colour. The yellow door links all the rooms together always directing you to the entrance. Two things to consider when planning a similar scenario:

- Consider your hallway with its function, use and the rooms surrounding it – how do they all relate?

- Can you see the door from all the different rooms or is it hidden with walls and furniture?

- Do you want to make a statement? Even choosing bronze or a similar material can create the same effect as this yellow door does, so thinking about impact and lasting effect is essential. Trend is an important factor to consider but also think of longevity of the colour in design and style.

In summary, door colour can be successful if thought out correctly. We have highlighted a few examples of colour throughout this book, go to Chapter 3; Hardwood Choices for Doors for more examples.

▶ 'Fun' would be the best word to describe this entrance hall and staircase. Royal blue, walnut wall cladding, and a concrete floor with art deco furniture – a recipe for success and always drawing the eye to the door somehow.

Natural finishes in different textures are only highlighted by the colour palette. A clever and challenging interior further elevated by the door.

CHEERAN HOUSE

THIS HOUSE SHOWS THE PRECISE DILEMMA FACING DESIGNERS WHEN TRYING TO CHOOSE A DOOR FOR A CONTEMPORARY NEW BUILD. WITH MORE THAN ONE MATERIAL ON THE FRONTAGE AND A PALETTE THAT NECESSITATES UNDERSTATEMENT, THE CHALLENGE ISN'T JUST GETTING THE DOOR RIGHT BUT ATTAINING THE OVERALL PRECISE OUTCOME OF UNASSUMING STYLE.

Designed as a courtyard house with a beautiful walled garden, the stark and minimalist interior allows for the garden and exterior to dominate. With the front door the only colour and real vivacious texture you can see internally, not going too over the top here was key.

As cube houses go this one has a distinct mood-chestnut cladding, flint faced walls, red brick, a sedum roof and anthracite grey windows. In contrast, the interior space is stark white with no additional finishes. With such a variety of finishes and textures, how do you choose a front door that highlights the entrance without compromising the mix of old and new to create this courtyard house?

- This is a particularly difficult house because the inside and out are so different. Texture on the outside and near none on the inside. Which is why the choice of hardwood here is probably the central predicament. Going darker in hue and as this hardwood changes in colour overtime –the overall effect intensifies the entrance area and gives importance where it's due. Iroko's colour is not too dark that it loses its warmth and not too brown to clash with the grey detail.

- Elegant and classic the front door design is simple and strong but not bold. The design is classic however some of the door elements (the fact it's a pivot door and large) means it fits into the contemporary cube style. Going for a vertical clad door also draws the eye up and elongates the door.

- Chestnut cladding is quite a popular choice due to its stability and it's ageing into silver grey over time. With the cladding and flint facing wall predominantly grey and the red brick walls, the front door had to stand out but not clash. Keeping these factors in mind and also the part of the house the door is being fitted onto helps make the right choices.

- One side lite keeps the entrance balanced with the rest of the building which leans to one side as part of the cube layout. Framing the door with that grey detail also accentuates the area.

- Using white internal doors throughout is another witty way to keep the front door distinct and individual. This is especially evident when there are other doors for storage or rooms right by the front door as in this case.

Elegance isn't that hard to achieve by thinking through all the seemingly trivial detail that could affect your decisions. Finish, texture, colour and layout are all part of that process.

◀▶ White and more white dominate here but the front door softens the severity and brings in the warmth where it's needed. Note that every door in the house other than the front door is white.

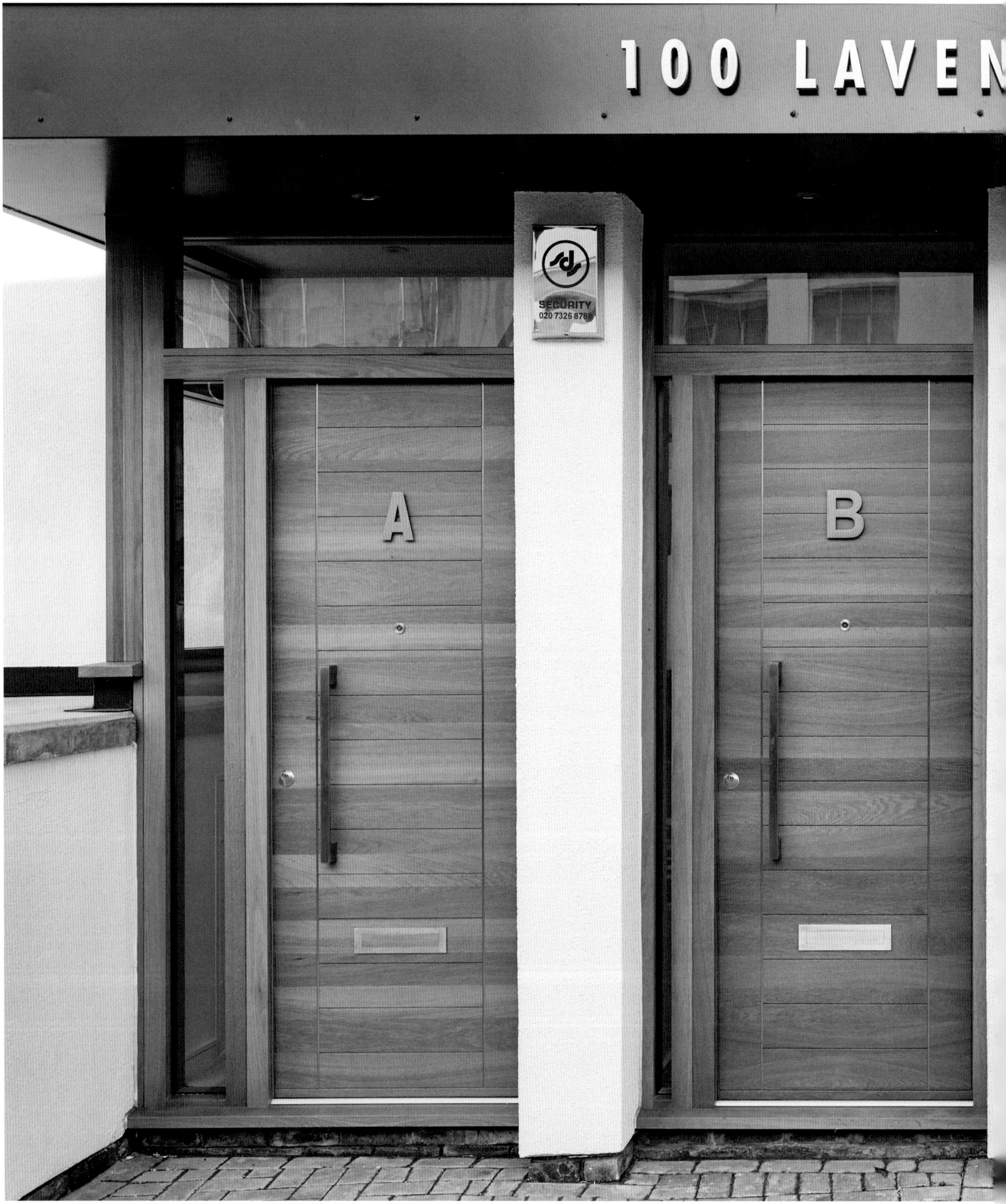
100 LAVEN
SECURITY
020 7326 878
A
B

CHAPTER EIGHT
DOORS FOR DEVELOPMENTS

DOORS FOR DEVELOPMENTS

IT WOULD BE ALL TOO EASY TO SUGGEST THAT DOORS IN DEVELOPMENTS SHOULD BE UNIFORM AND CORRESPOND WITH EACH OTHER TO CREATE HARMONY.
QUITE THE REVERSE, DEVELOPMENTS VARY CONSIDERABLY AND IT DEPENDS ON THE NATURE OF THE DEVELOPMENT. EIGHT DIFFERENT DEVELOPMENTS HAVE BEEN CHOSEN TO USE AS EXAMPLES FOR THIS CHAPTER WITH FOUR SIGNIFICANT AREAS TO CONCENTRATE ON INCLUDING SIZE, BUDGET, DESIGN AND LOCATION.

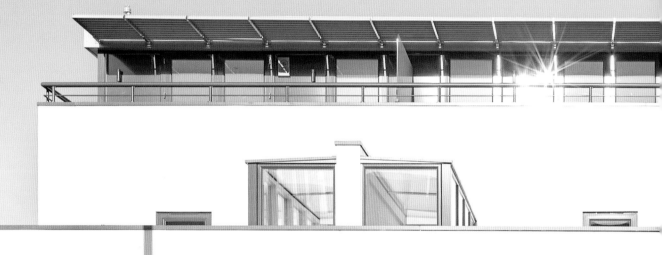

This development is an impressive example of homogeneity. Mirrored doors along the frontage with matching accessories and a clear identity.

100 LAVENDER HILL

◀ Themes work. The brick wall continues through the hallways and indicates how important it is to ensure front doors look just as good from the inside.

When we think of size, you may think of the size of each individual house/apartment or of the size of the development itself. Some developments could comprise only two one off houses compared to a large development of say fifty houses or more. The size of each house can be relevant in terms of sale price and differentiation whereas the size of the development can have a bearing in terms of whether uniformity is essential.

Differentiation, in this case, is to give some houses on a development an edge. This could work for detached houses when there are say some semi-detached and terrace houses and apartments. Giving the detached houses something more substantial in terms of quality and design creates status and helps with sales price.

The examples in this chapter concentrate on developments where uniformity rules.
However, simple changes like changing handles, adding a side lite or a vision panel or even swapping the way the door opens creates some differentiation between each house. Changing the colour of the door even if it's the same design can do the job too. Maybe only the finish is the same for all the doors on the same development and everything else is different, but this still works because there is one shared factor.

The role that location plays is slightly different as it could be interpreted two ways. The location of the development geographically (near a beach, countryside or town) and the location of the development itself in terms of prestige (i.e. location, location, location) which also relates to budget and design choices. Choosing a door for a development isn't only about budget but it is a necessary evil.

▲ Black on black adds depth and a stylish edge which helps highlight the oak bench area.

▶ Uniformity works well for this development with its light coloured brick, charred cladding and dark grey windows. What's interesting is that the developer has opted for the oak cladding by the door to stand out instead of the door. A genuinely clever way to keep the maintenance low.

A look through from one door to another. Standardising the look throughout keeps everything consistent and budgets low.

▶ The move to a more contemporary design for developments shows the importance of detail like concrete floors and paired down finishes. This shot of the show home highlights the importance of doors from the inside and out in addition to subtle colours and giving the impression of space.

▼ Every house on this development follows
a U shape blueprint with an emphasis of
differentiation focused on the front door areas.
The house below has more glass than the
others and that helps break the strong stone
cladding. The front door appears to be a
double door but is actually a door and
a boarded side panel.

▲ The internal view of this doorway works very well because the door is not central and therefore adds interest. This configuration hides that part of the hallway for privacy so it's possible to come to the door and not be seen.

Note how the door design remains the same for all the houses but the entrance design itself is what is different. The doorways look exclusive and whether they are configured with one side lite or two or with a boarded panel, each house demands its own individuality. The softness of the Iroko wood balances out the stone cladding and all of it matches well with the grey slate roof.

▲ Using etched glass in the side lites softens the light and provides privacy all at once. Matching the internal doors in finish and an all-white interior work well to highlight the front door too.

▼ Using a door with vertical cladding instead
of matching it to the existing horizontal
cladding gives the door some power.
No way you can escape that it's the front door.
Choosing a shade lighter is also a clever way
to stand out.

▲ On this development in Bristol, some
of the doors have side lites and some don't.
This helps distinguish the more expensive
and larger homes.

◀ There are various benefits to choosing a painted door for a development like this one in Bristol. Painted doors need less maintenance over time, and the internal view works just as well as the façade with whitewashed oak floors and stark white walls.

▼ Note how all the accessories work together to create a harmonious and contemporary looking entrance. An all grey door stands out against all the wooden cladding which will eventually grey and weather. Choosing doors that work in the future as well as the present can help keep a development up to date and new.

▶ Location has determined the design of the doors for these two distinct houses. Keeping it simple with an understated door design was fundamental to performance over time and to the style of the buildings. Sand and the potential weathering determine the overall design aesthetic and spend.

◀ With only four houses in this development, the doors aren't visible from the road but no less important. Here the designer has matched the doors with the overhead cladding to the entrance side. This shows how different materials work well together to create an overall impression.

An old church is developed into two houses with matching doors on either side of the building. The challenge here was to find a door that was in keeping but helped to create a homely feel.

◀ In this development, two door designs have been used to create differentiation and for the simple reason of introducing more light.

The choice of oak gives the doors identity and helps them stand out in an otherwise white and grey facade.

Keeping the doors in the same oak finish and horizontally boarded to match the cladding brings the scheme together.

PHOTOGRAPHY

ANDY STAGG

A London based photographer specialising in the documentation of architecture and design. He creates images through the processes of composition, lighting and focused observation. His images translate an experience of the character and atmosphere of a project and its position within the fabric of community and landscape.

Andy's work on the book images was always door focused slightly changing his usual perspective on architecture alone. His eye for detail and his ability to capture the right light, feeling and atmosphere of the buildings is superb. He places importance on every angle and gives every door and building an identity and frame that you would never have thought of. Thank you Andy for making this book look as good as it does.

Please note: There are only 3 images by other photographers in this book and these have an asterisk next to their names in the projects section. These are Matt Porteus, Heiko Prigge and James Ram.

PROJECTS

Disclaimer: Where possible and the information has been available, we have identified the key architects and developers of the projects in this book.

1. Oakwright *p.11,12,111,123*

2. Osbourne Developments *p.14,47,129,130*

3. Lorna McNeals *p.15,137*

4. Living in Space *p.16,162*

Photography: Andy Stagg

PROJECTS

Photography: Andy Stagg

PROJECTS

Photography: Andy Stagg
*Matt Porteus **Heiko Prigge

PROJECTS

Photography: Andy Stagg

GLOSSARY

Aluminium curtain walling – A curtain wall system is an outer covering of a building in which the walls are non-structural. Curtain-wall systems are designed with extruded aluminum members and are usually made of glass, specialist panelling or stone.

Cill –the cill of a doorway is a horizontal piece of timber that forms the bottom part of the door and provides support for the door sometimes at a structural level. The cill usually holds the threshold of the door which in turn holds the weather seals.

CNC machine –CNC stands for Computer Numerical Control and is a term used in the manufacturing sector to explain a machine that uses a computer to control tools. Some of the tools used are routers and grinders.

Cylinder lock – The cylinder lock is where you put the key to open a door, and is a lock in which a cylinder rotates to move a bolt; inserting the key lifts and aligns the pins to free the cylinder to rotate.

Door leaf – the part of a door that constitutes the door panel only before it is swung and before it is fitted with any door furniture.

Door set- a fully assembled unit which includes a door leaf, all door furniture and frames and is ready for fitting.

Elevation – in architecture, the elevation is the front, side or back of a building or a drawing of one of these elements.

Escutcheon – is a protective surround for the cylinder lock and can prevent access or tidy up the area around the cylinder lock.

Fail secure/ fail safe Fail secure means that if the power fails, the door remains secure (locked). Fail safe means the opposite: if power fails, the door is unlocked.

Latch multipoint lock – a lock includes a centrally located deadbolt, a latch and at least 2 bolts or hook bolts ie a minimum of 3points of locking

Pivot hinges – are typically used on larger doors where the middle part of the door is in alignment with the pivot hinges at the top and bottom of the door. The operation itself allows the door to function on a barrel so that the hollow cylinder allows for a rotational bearing force.

Self-locking –a device for securing a door consisting of a bolt or system of bolts propelled and withdrawn by a mechanism operated by a key once the door shuts.

Side lite a glass panel next to a door.

Storeylite a glass panel above a door.

3D hinges are hinges for side hung doors that allow you to adjust the door in three different positions upwards, downwards and sideways.

Even when the front door is hidden on the front elevation like this one, it's still possible to make an entrance of a front door. This works because of the angle of the walls on either side, the height of the door and the choice of timber. The door remains protected from the elements as well.

INDEX

THE AUTHOR

Elizabeth Assaf is an authority on door design. She has worked in door design and manufacturing for over 15 years and is the company director of Urban Front; a business which specialises in contemporary hardwood steel reinforced doors. Elizabeth has helped create doors to adorn hundreds of exceptional properties across the UK, Europe and further afield. Now she wants to share her expertise, knowledge and experience through Door Couture.

Elizabeth has previously worked on television shows Property Ladder and Changing Rooms, where her passion for interior design blossomed. Identifying a gap in the market for contemporary doors, Elizabeth successfully launched Urban Front with her husband, Nabil, in 2003. Urban Front has become a market leader and as a result, Elizabeth has written and delivered RIBA certified CPD, written articles for magazines and been involved in many international endeavours - including designing and making a door for the residence of the British Consulate in New York.

ACKNOWLEDGEMENTS

First, I'd like to thank Rachel Davies from RIBA it was her suggestion to write this book. She planted the seed and I was hooked. In addition to Gemma Dart for answering all my questions. Huge thanks to Chris from Self-Publishing Success, I would have never had the courage to self publish this book without his words of wisdom.

A big thank you to my colleagues James Barnard and Tyrone McDowall for all their support and help with the details. Victoria Bowcock spent a lot of time changing and improving the layouts and I thank her for all of her hard work; especially being patient with me when I had literally no idea what I was doing! Pooja Ramavrat for doing the final proofread.

A shout out as well to Joe Gregory, Rethink Press for all his support and help.

Jane Duncan who has been a great supporter of our company and for writing a wonderful forward.

My brother Pierre Issa for all his help with ideas and just generally being there for me. My mother Jimali McKihnon who has always been my biggest fan. My parents Michael and Therese for their support from afar.

My wonderful husband Nabil who has supported me every step of the way with information and checking and rechecking my work and making sure that all of my technical detail was correct.

Finally Naomi Cleaver, Oliver Heath and Heinz Richardson for their amazing reviews.